Chillin' in the Stroma

by Joe Rue

RoseDog Books
PITTSBURGH, PENNSYLVANIA 15238

RoseDog Books
585 Alpha Drive
Pittsburgh, PA 15238
Visit our website at *www.rosedogbookstore.com*

ISBN: 979-8-8892-5271-9
eISBN: 979-8-8892-5771-4

Chillin' in the Stroma

This book is dedicated to all my students
who inspired me over the years.

Introduction

This book is not a biology book explaining different processes and biological events as the title might imply, but it is a compilation of different stories and situations that happened to me in my close to forty years as a teacher…actually my sixty-seven years as a person. Most stories will have me as the central protagonist, but other tales will indirectly deal with me.

I will include conversations and exchanges I encountered with acquaintances and friends and even complete strangers. Some of these encounters made a mark on me, and in some cases, hopefully, helped others.

For example one day a colleague approached me and asked, "Joe, are your students bored in class; I think they are bored in my class?"

I then asked him, "Are you excited with your lessons?"

He replied, " No, I'm bored." Well that explained that.

I told him, "We are like the storytellers of old who would tell tales around the bonfire. Tell stories that relate to the topics covered. Tell interesting stories. Make them relatable." When preparing a class, I always ask myself if I, as a young Joey Rue, would enjoy the class. Would I be entertained? To be honest, I believe my students are entertained while I present to them complex material in biology sprinkled with interesting facts and often humorous stories.

So recently I was in class, and one of my students raised his hand

and said, "Mr. Rue, you have such amazing stories, you should write a book." I guess that was the start, the seed that would eventually germinate into ***Chillin' in The Stroma***.

Chillin' in the Stroma…what a curious title for a book. Ironically the title appeared before I even wrote one word of the book. When I taught photosynthesis, I explained the light dependent reaction and the light independent phase. I talked about three carbon molecules called PGA, or phosphoglyceric acid waiting in the stroma, the liquid part of the chloroplast, for the high energy molecules coming from the light phase. I would say that these molecules were chilling in the stroma… just waiting. One year I said chilling in the stroma had a very cool ring to it, and if I ever wrote a book, that would be the title. So here it is, ***Chillin' in the Stroma***. Ironically this is the last time you will hear the word stroma again in this book. Instead we will hear stories and life-experiences. I hope you find these interesting and fun and, in some cases, funny. I will try to be as faithful to the stories as possible. What I explain in these stories really did happen. A funny thing happened along the way where I have seen someone telling one of my stories, appropriating parts of a story and claiming it to be their own when in fact it wasn't. Other times some have retold one of my stories about me but with a very different development. The story evolved over time with multiple tellings. I'm not saying any of this was done maliciously, but the mind can play funny tricks on us. I will attempt to be as faithful to these stories and avoid any deviations from the truth. So sit back and enjoy the many tales of my life.

The Valbanera

Many a time my sister Flora and I would sit with my dad and hear stories of the past. One that stood out was a story of my grandparents' immigration to Cuba from Spain in 1919. Back then a transatlantic voyage would take a long time and usually would entail staying at your destination for various years. So my grandparents departed from Barcelona destined for La Havana to visit a brother and start a new life. They sailed on a ship called La Valbanera, making stops in Puerto Rico and Santiago de Cuba before reaching La Havana. As it turned out, when my grandparents were docked in Santiago, they received a telegram from the brother saying that it was more convenient for him to pick them up at Santiago instead of Havana because he was completing some business near Santiago. So my grandparents disembarked leaving La Valbanera behind before it departed for Havana. The weather was getting worse at the time, and by the time La Valbanera reached La Havana, the harbor was closed due to an impending hurricane. The captain decided to ride out the storm in open sea, hoping to keep the ship safe. But that was not meant to be. La Valbanera faced the full force of the hurricane and sank. There were no survivors. My dad told me this story quite a few times, but I forgot the name of the ship until he mentioned it the year before he passed away. I remember him sitting in the living room couch chair, telling the story and mentioning the name of the ship. It stuck with me because of its curious name. After he passed away, I decided to look up the story in the Internet to see if anyone had more information on the Valbanera. I was surprised to find out this was a very famous case at the time, in fact they called it the Spanish Titanic, being the worst Spanish non-wartime merchant marine disaster. On September 9th, 1919, La Valbanera sank some 200 kms from its original destination, some ten kms off Key West, only twelve meters down in an area called Half Moon Bank, the Quicksands. There were some mysteries linked to this tragedy. Four-hundred-eighty-eight people died, but for the longest time no bodies or remains were found there or elsewhere. Eventually divers found a single head in the wreckage. Another strange fact from studying the wreck was that no life boats were launched. Spooked by a young girl who had a premonition that the ship would sink, 736 passengers, the majority with tickets to Havana disembarked in Santiago. Whatever the reason was, those who left La Valbanera in Santiago were saved from a mysterious death. I think that if it weren't for that telegram asking my grandparents to disembark, my grandparents would not have survived, my dad would not have been born, and I would not be here writing this book.

https://www.florida-keys-vacation.com › *Valbanera https.www. Enigmas del mundo – El Valbanera (El Titanic Espanol)*
https://www.florida-keys-vacation.com › Valbanera.html
https://www.coolturalanzarote.com › en › the-greatest-spanish-naval-tragedy-in-times-of-peace-

The Smuggler

So, as you already know, my dad enjoyed sharing his past with us. And his past was quite florid. He underwent many adventures and he lived a very exciting life. He shared with us stories of how he was a smuggler across the border of Spain and France usually going through Andorra. I have to say, as a kid, I was mesmerized by these stories and I would like it when he would share these stories with my friends. But as I grew older, I started to prefer he would not share these with my friends. It was like my dad was a pirate….a smuggler. And then I had my concerns about his smuggling activities.

So one day, I came out and asked him, "What things did you smuggle?" He replied perfumes, silk, food, jewelry. It was a time when average people had shortage of things, and my dad would supply these items.

"There were two things I would never smuggle. Drugs and guns," he told me. That reply put me at ease.

One day I asked him what I thought to be an unrelated question "Pop, why did you lose your toenails?" I was surprised that the response went back to his smuggling days. Without giving it much importance, he told me that once he had smuggled not clothes, nor alcohol, nor cigarettes; he had smuggled a Jewish family from France to Spain. There were checkpoints in the mountains, but my dad knew the officers, and he would usually pay them off with a bottle of whiskey or some clothing item.

That time when he approached the checkpoint, one of the guards he knew came out and shouted, "Halt." He was actually warning my dad. This guard exited The Guard House, but there was another officer who was not known to my father, and he took some pot shots at my dad and the family. He ran with them through the woods, eventually finding a frozen stream. My dad directed them into the water, and they remained in the water avoiding the guards. They eventually found their way to Spain, and the family was safe, but my dad got frostbite in his toes, losing his toenails. After hearing that story, I remember being very proud of my father.

D-Day

My uncle Ben Campo was one of my mother's siblings. They were Margaret, Ben, Mary (my mother), and Angelo. In 1944 Ben went to England uniting with some 150,000 British, Canadian, American, Australian, and other soldiers waiting for the great invasion. On June 6th, the landing on Normandy took place. Decades later Steven Spielberg depicted the D-Day Landings with great realism. In 1998 I was watching *Saving Private Ryan* in a local theater when I noticed an elderly gentleman across the aisle crying during the battle scenes. He was obviously recalling horrors from the past. Some believe that over 4,000 Allied troops perished during the invasion and thousands more were wounded. Among these injured was my Uncle Ben. During the beach landing, most likely at Omaha Beach, my uncle was injured losing an eye. He remained in a military hospital before returning home to Montpellier, Vermont. He eventually went to Spain, where Margaret was living, and he married a Spanish señorita, Encarnita. In 1960 my father, my mother, my sister, Flora and I went to spend some time that summer in Madrid. So off we went from Brooklyn to spend the summer in Spain. Regretfully, during my first encounter with Spain, I came down with Scarlet Fever, also known as Scarlatina. I couldn't go sightseeing with my family and I stayed in bed over my aunt's house. It was this time when my uncle Ben dropped over various times to keep me company. He told me stories of his stay in England and his fellow soldiers. He told war stories, which most I cannot remember now because I was too young. He sang an old song from those days, "Don't sit under the apple tree with anyone else but me…" Then he gave me a spoon and said that he wanted to show me something.

He then said, "Gently, hit my eye." What? "Don't worry, Joey, you won't hurt me" So I went with the spoon for the eye. My uncle said, "Woah, make sure you hit the right eye." And when I did, I heard a ching like when you make a toast with glass cups. When I touched his glass eye, it chimed. I will never forget that. That was my introduction to Uncle Benny's glass eye, his souvenir from Normandy.

Decades later my uncle peacefully passed away sitting in his lounge chair. Another decade past and there was a robbery in his house and the thieves stole his Purple Heart. We tried to get it replaced, but the military said their records were damaged and they couldn't replace it. That's a pity since it would have been a wonderful family heirloom.

My final connection with D-Day was in 2019 when I went with my nephew David to visit the beaches of Normandy. We saw the beaches: Gold, Juno, Sword, and Utah. There were over 2,000 American casualties at Omaha Beach alone. We went to the American cemetery and were impressed by a sea of white crosses and stars. This was a reflection of the great endeavor launched to stop a major evil. And my Uncle Ben was a part of it.

https://www.cdc.gov
https://www.history.com › topics › world-war-ii › d-day

Frogs

I was ten-years-old and I spent part of the summer over my aunt's house in the mountains. There were hills and valleys and a little stream where we could swim. I loved playing around in this natural setting, though I longed for friends my age. Then one day I met another boy, and we hit it off. He seemed like a very nice kid and he said he would introduce me to other kids. So a few days later, he introduced me to another three boys. We laughed and had a fun time. Then one of the boys said they wanted to show me something special. Great! I thought.

They brought a straw basket with them and said, "Now go fill the basket with frogs." There were plenty of frogs along the hills and stream. I thought this was going to be awesome. Maybe have a frog race or line them up by size and play with them. It was getting late and it was getting dark. So we gathered around the straw basket, and one boy explained what we were doing. He had a small bottle with some flammable liquid in it. He then squirted the liquid in a spiral, making its way to the center where the basket was with the frogs. He explained that then he would light the flammable liquid, which would make its way to the basket, lighting up the frogs. This has to be a joke! I thought. As the fire approached the frogs, I realized the frogs were going to burn. I couldn't let these poor creatures suffer. I then gave a shout, and like a possessed madman, I jumped in and kicked the basket as far as I could liberating the frogs. I was pleased seeing the frogs run off to freedom and safety. The other boys were upset because their experiment was messed up because of the new kid.

"You missed the point, Joe," they angrily said. Inside I thought, I definitely got the point. Needless to say, I was never invited to hang out with this group of misguided kids…and that was fine by me. Before I knew it, my summer stay with my aunt was over. For the most part, I had a fun time…and I saved around a dozen frogs along the way.

Nuns

In Brooklyn I grew up in the bosom of the Catholic Church, surrounded by stained glass, statues, religious holidays, priests, and nuns. I always felt that these were holy. Especially nuns. And movies reinforced my concept of nuns, movies such as *The Sound of Music, Heaven Knows Mr. Allison, The Nun's Story, Where Angels Go, Trouble Follows, Black Orpheus,* and *Sister Act.* All these films brought me back to my first grade with Sister Joseph. Back then she was one of the nicest people I had encountered in my seven years on this planet. I found myself admiring her clean hands and face and her tidy habit. Her black and white habit reminded me of a friendly and loving penguin. She had a bright smile and a jovial personality. No, I didn't know much about going out with someone being seven and all, but I gave it much thought and I knew what I had to do. So I mustered up all my energy and courage and I approached Sister Joseph.

I asked her, "Sister Joseph, may I speak with you?"

She replied with a gentleness, "Yes, Joseph, what is it?"

"Well, Sister, I've given this much thought and I decided I want to marry you."

"Well this is a surprise," she said. I wondered, *I'm not sure how to go about this and how to get the wedding prepared, but I am convinced that I want to do this.* She had a pleasant smile on her face, though she was not condescending nor was she making fun of my request.

"Joseph, I appreciate your offer, but it is impossible because I am already married." She showed me her ring. I remained there quite confused. She was a nun, how can she be married? "Joseph, I am married to Jesus."

I was in a state of shock, "So let me get this straight, you cannot marry me because you are already married to Jesus?"

"That's right, thank you for your offer. It is flattering, but I cannot marry you," she said. I remember leaving her office broken hearted, I ran home and started to cry.

My mother opened the door, and her first reaction was to say, "Who hit you?" When I told her, I realized she was doing her best not to laugh and to encourage me. "You will find someone else who is not a nun. Now, love, you go play with your friends." And that was my last proposal to a nun.

A second world shattering encounter with a nun was when I was around twelve-years-old and I was asked to drop by the convent to help with a house chore the nuns needed help with. When I pressed the doorbell, Sister Andrews opened the door, but then it happened. Under her veil, a locket of her hair was peeping out. Oh my gosh! I didn't know for sure what the ruling was, but the nuns must hide their hair for a reason. In fact this was probably a mortal sin. So I thought that I mustn't look at this rebellious lock of hair.

I started looking down and looking away, and she asked, "Joseph, are you alright?"

"Yes, Sister, what do you want me to help you with?" It was something about the window, but to tell you the truth, I don't exactly remember what it was. It was difficult getting around the convent while avoiding seeing Sister Andrews' hair and doing my best to avoid a mortal sin. A few years later, things became easier when nuns started showing their hair without the veil.

My final encounter with a nun was when I was volunteering in a shelter. There was this young woman who also volunteered. The truth was that she didn't interact much with me. In fact she seemed to be quite serious. One day I saw her very happy and pleasant and I asked her what was making her so happy.

She replied, "Tomorrow I am heading off to a very special place upstate New York."

I said, "Why don't you write me let me know how it is."

She said, "I can't."

"OK, give me your address and I'll write you."

"We can't do that either."

"Why?" I asked.

"Because I'm going to be in a cloister where I cannot contact people outside nor write them."

"So if this is your last night, why don't we go out and have dinner as a going away present," she agreed. She was so pleasant and nice, and I asked her why she had to be a cloister nun.

"Couldn't you be a nun and continue working with the poor?"

She replied, "I can do more good with my prayers and being in contact with Jesus." We had a delightful dinner. We laughed and had a very happy time. We finished with an enjoyable conversation over coffee and dessert. I dropped her off and said goodnight. I never saw her nor heard from her again. Now I wonder how she's doing, but I hope she is as happy as the last day I saw her. Even more so.

World's Fair

1964 was the year of the New York World's Fair. Well actually it was the third New York World's Fair. The first two were in 1853, then 1939. Both the 1939 and the 1964 were located in Flushing Meadows, Queens. When I pass by now and I see the Giant Unisphere, which was the symbol of the '64 World's Fair, I still think of the happy times going to the fair. I remember being ten and going with my family to this magical fair that propelled us from the past into the future: from the Hall of Presidents to the Home of the Future. There were space rockets and giant Ferris wheels. One of the pavilions I remember most was Pepsi Cola's. It's a Small World, a Disney inspired ride seeing dolls from all over the globe in their traditional clothing while a memorable song played on. It's a Small World After All, It's a Small World After All, It's a Small World After All, It's a Small, Small World! Another Disney inspired ride was GE's Progressland with another catchy song, "There's a Great Big Beautiful Tomorrow." When the fair finished both of these pavilions were taken to Disney World as permanent exhibits.

There were pavilions, which offered culture to all visitors. I was impressed by Michelangelo's Pieta on loan from the Vatican, the Watusi dancers from Africa who jumped high in the sky, and Flamenco dancers in the Spanish Pavilion. Being a fan of the historical figure, El Cid, I was excited to see his two authentic swords, Colada and Tizona. There were many appearances of popular or soon to be popular items. For example here was the first time I saw people throwing frisbees and doing a demonstration that seemed like magic. It was the first time I saw a jet pack man fly in the sky, a precursor to 007's flight in Thunderball. It was the first time I went with my family to the franchise, TAD's Steakhouse. Throughout the fair, there were machines that for a quarter would make wax dinosaurs, which I, of course, collected a multitude of these prehistoric creatures. Here was also my introduction to a Spanish treat called "churros." Every time I went to the fair (a total of ten times), I was sure to munch on churros.

Another thrill was going to the New York City Pavilion and seeing the New York Panorama, a model of all of New York where every house was represented. It was exciting to find your house in this giant representation. All in all, going to the 1964 World's Fair was an unforgettable time.

https://blog.genealogybank.com > 1964-worlds-fair-history-photos-memorabilia.html

5th Grade

I was ten-years-old when my family decided to leave Brooklyn and head over to live in Spain. That was my second time to Spain after my summer with scarlet fever. But Spain was like a paradise. It was a great opportunity for us since everything was so very cheap. For example we could have a three-course meal with dessert and coffee (which I didn't partake of) for a measly dollar or two. My dad felt that we could live like kings with what he had saved up. The family talked it over, and we all decided to give it a shot. When we got to Madrid, my parents asked me what would I want, to sign up to a Spanish school and learn the language or to go to an American school and take much longer to master the language. I always took the bull by the horns. It was like learning how to swim by being tossed into the pool.

I said, "I'll try the Spanish school." So on my first day, I was faced with an entrance test for the fifth-grade. But it was in Spanish, and I hardly understood a word. I do remember, however, one question, "Cual es la montaña más alta de España?" Montaña sounded like mountain, and España was Spain, so I figured out that they were asking me which is the tallest mountain of Spain, but I didn't know the answer. Now I know it to be the Teide Mountain. The next day, they read the results out in class: Juan Rodriguez 96%, Pedro Sanchez 89%, Felipe Fernandez 93%...Joseph Rue 2%. There was absolute silence. Nobody laughed, but they all looked at me as if I were a special case. They made me take the entrance test for fourth-grade. I failed that. Then I took the test for third-grade. I also failed that. Then I failed the test for second-grade, then first, then kindergarten. At this point, I started crying.

"Please find someone who speaks English." A young priest met up with me, and I cried out, "Father, I can't go back to kindergarten. I was always at the top of my class. Help me please." We spoke for a while.

At this point, the priest said something like, "This boy isn't stupid, he just doesn't speak Spanish." So I was placed back in the fifth-grade and I started my adventure to learn Spanish. Little by little, I started to master Español. Day after day, I struggled to learn this language, and with patience and perseverance, I learned. By the end of the year, we had an all-school assembly where they announced the results of a school wide spelling bee competition.

When the principal announced the top three students in the school, he started by saying, "I don't know whether to feel embarrassed or incredibly proud of our third winner. This young man started the year not knowing any Spanish and finished the year having taken third place in our school wide spelling bee." Needless to say, that was me. By the end of the school year, I must admit I mastered Spanish, but my family returned to New York. Why? Well that story is for another chapter.

A Sickly Specimen

The truth is I was a pretty sickly boy growing up in Brooklyn. I had asthma, which made me weaker than the average boy. I couldn't run fast, especially in cold weather, which would induce an asthma attack. But this helped me to grow up being patient and resilient. My mom often told a story of one day when she heard me talking with someone up on the second floor. She came up the stairs to see who I was talking to and went to my room. Though the cracked opening in the door, she saw me speaking to a little crucifix I owned.

"Jesus, don't get me wrong, I'm not complaining, but why can't I be like other children running and playing outside?" That was a heart-breaking moment for my mother. But I continued seeing a doctor once a week, taking antibiotic shots as a precaution not to get an infection in my lung. I recall one incident where my dad brought home a parakeet named Jack. Now Jack would scratch a lot and his dander set off an asthma attack, not allowing me to breathe, inducing my folks to call the emergency room. When the EMS arrived to my house, they put me on the dining room table and made a tent over me, which they filled with vapors to open up my bronchioles and allow me to breathe. They said they had to deal with this and we wouldn't have time to rush to the hospital. Back then we didn't have the use of inhalers like we do today. In 1965 my family moved to Spain, but my sickly nature continued the year that I was in Spain. I got various sicknesses. First hepatitis. I believe I got this eating bad seafood. I was in bed for over a month, my skin had this yellow appearance referred to as jaundice. By the time I was cured, I had lost much weight and I was quite weak. It was around Easter time when I got pneumonia. I remember the doctor would come to my house, roll me over, and give me a shot, which was meant to clear up my bronchial passages. When I got over pneumonia, I got a flu. Then another flu, then another, and my family was quite concerned that I was not going to make it, so we decided to return to America to see if I could recuperate. My mom jokingly said one American hot dog, and I was cured. The truth is I was outgrowing my weak nature getting stronger in my teens. By the time I was in high school, I was like the average American boy from that point on. I was healthy. In fact I didn't need to go to the hospital or see a doctor until my mid-forties with a hernia operation. My weak health was a thing of the past…and of the future.

Flora

My sister, Flora, has been a most important part of my life. She would always have my back, and I would know who to see if I had a problem. I knew she always loved me and was protective of her little brother. I remember the day my buddy Joe Murno dropped over my house to see if I wanted to go to the beach with him. His older sister was driving. I agreed, but I failed to tell anybody that I was going. We went to the beach, had a good time, and came home after three hours. As we arrived to my house, I saw my sister in front of the house crying. What happened, I asked. You were missing, and we had no idea where you were. I felt like a real cad. Flora always looked after me. I remember vividly the year I was in Spain and sick with hepatitis, my sister had been with friends to the movies. I couldn't go, and this was before the technology of VHS. I was feeling down that I missed the movie, but I remember Flora took me into her room, sat me down, and started telling me the whole movie. It was a western, and the main character was playing off of two rival families. Eventually they realized this, and they beat him to a pulp. He managed to escape, crawling like a snake under floorboards. When he healed, he returned and had a showdown with the main villain. After he headed off to the sunset. Fini. I had a vivid image of this western hero, or better yet antihero. For the longest time, I wanted to see this movie, which I had imagined in my head. As you probably already surmised, the film was a rehash of the Japanese movie *Yojimbo*. This western starred a young American actor called Clint Eastwood, and the movie was *A Fistful of Dollars*. Flora's patience and caring was reflected in her willingness to help her sickly brother.

We often talk about a connection that we have. On many occasions, I picked up the phone to call her in Spain, and instantly she would be on the line because she was calling me with the same intentions. These were uncanny coincidences. The strangest event happened one year when she was waiting a few hours for a transfer at JFK. She had phoned me and had asked me to meet her and a few of her friends there, but I told her I couldn't because I was working. As it turned out, I finished early and I decided to surprise her. As I approached this long corridor at the TWA terminal, I saw Flora waiting for me.

"But I told you I couldn't come. Why are you waiting for me?" She then told me she was talking with her friends and suddenly said, "I have to go meet my brother." Her friends reminded her that I couldn't make it. To which she replied, "Yes, but he's here now." When I showed up, her friends were incredulous.

Throughout the years, she has always been there for me: from typing out my thesis to organizing my travel plans, I have been blessed with the greatest sister one could ever ask for. And you know what, she still is the best.

Scab

The seventies was quite a tumultuous time in Spain. There was some political unrest as Francisco Franco, the dictator of Spain, died in the mid-seventies, and there were protests in the university. I often felt the seventies in Spain were like the sixties in America, a very political period. My time in the Autonoma University was quite an experience. I found myself flung into the mix without even realizing it.

One day I was late to class. I went running, and there was a large group of students in front of my classroom. I wondered what they were doing there, but I couldn't stop. I was late to class. I passed everyone and went inside. To my surprise, we were only seven students when usually there would be over sixty. I asked one of the other students what was happening, but I didn't get much of a reply. The teacher came in, thanked us for being there, and started the class with only seven while dozens were outside chanting and shouting.

"What was happening?" Then the students crashed into the classroom and literally kicked the teacher out. Then they faced the seven who were in the class and started shouting and insulting us. As it turns out, we broke the picket line and entered the class. We were scabs. I was straight from an American high school where I never worried about picket lines and riots. Furthermore I wasn't even fully aware of what the issue and the complaints were. Supposedly there was a young man who was shot in a different region of Spain, and the students in Madrid were protesting. I probably would not have crossed the picket line if I were totally aware of the situation, but I wasn't.

So there I was sitting in the classroom with another six students who passed the picket line, hearing all the shouting when one student who was the head of the student Communist party shouted out, "You are all sons of bitches, especially the American son of a bitch." Many of the people there stopped shouting and looked at me to see what I would do because this attack was personal. I couldn't believe this was happening. Many of the students were classmates who were just there to see what was happening. They didn't want this either. I didn't know what to do. My brain wasn't functioning right. I stood up and changed my seat. Why? I have no idea, I just felt so uncomfortable in that chair with everyone looking at me. There was absolutely no logic to why I got up and changed my seat. Then there was a commotion, and the riot police with their visors down and their Billi sticks came charging in.

One approached me and said, "Time to leave, kid." I originally didn't want to leave my seat. I was glued to it. He said, "Last warning, kid, get out now." I did, considering I wasn't even sure what I was doing there in the first place.

On the way out, I found the head of the communist who said to me, "I'm not that angry at you because you have balls and you stand up for what you believe." Stand up for what I believe in…what is he talking about? I accidentally went in the class because I was late. The seven students who crossed the picket line became somewhat of a notorious group. People were talking about us as if we stood for something. I know some of the seven crossed the picket line intentionally because they were fed up with all the politics in the university. I didn't. I just didn't want to be late to class.

A week later, I was taking the bus from the University and I started chatting with this girl next to me. She asked me if I heard about the commotion in the school of science?

"Did you hear that there was this American who jumped on the head of the communist and fought his way through the crowd of students." I said that sounded very heroic, but I told her that wasn't quite what happened. "What do you mean?" she asked, somewhat annoyed because I was contradicting her story.

"Well the American didn't attack anybody, he just moved around his seat."

"That's ridiculous, besides my brother was there and he saw it all."

"Wow." I then told her that's not what happened. "I should know because I'm the American, I was the only American there."

"Well you're wrong because my brother was there." So the story went on being embellished as it was told from person to person….so I single-handedly jumped the crowd like a crazed warrior. One thing that did come out of this strange event was that I became very close friends with the other six. As it turned out, not all of them were making a political stand either. We weren't scabs, we were just college freshman wanting to attend our class.

Tatum & Beadle

This is a story I share with my students when talking about procrastinating. When I was in college in Madrid, one week I was assigned to prepare a four-page paper on Beadle and Tatum's report on one gene corresponding to one protein. I had all week to prepare it, and on Friday of that week, I had to present it to a small group of Geneticists. Since it was a very busy week for me, I waited till Thursday night to prepare my talk. Just as I was about to start my preparation, I received a call.

"Joe, you'll never believe it, but I got two tickets for the Spanish premiere of the sci-fi movie that is breaking all records in the US."

"You don't mean the movie with big, hairy creatures, robots, and laser battles?" I inquired. Yes, it was the Spanish premiere of ...*Star Wars!* I couldn't pass this opportunity by. So I met up with my friend to see the 10:30 P.M. showing. By the time I returned home, it was real late, and I was very tired. I was too tired to start preparing my presentation, but I had a free before my presentation anyway. So the next day, I tackled the four-page paper. I mean four pages, how hard can that be? Have you ever read a paragraph and it was so dense, you had to reread it and then reread it again and then reread it one more time? Well that was what happened to me. It was like reading a paragraph in Swahili. It just didn't penetrate my brain. My free period was over, and it was time to give my presentation. But I thought it was OK, "I'll just wing it. After all, whatever challenge I faced, I would overcome it and come out with flying colors." So I began. Everyone was quiet and attentive. I even thought, "This must be turning out quite good since there were no questions." When I finished, I asked if anyone had any questions.

The key professor said, "I just have one question…Are you stupid, or are you just acting stupid?" A rush of adrenalin went through my body. I was in a situation of extreme crisis. This can't be happening to me. But it didn't stop there. He proceeded to ask me multiple questions, uncovering any weakness. I got so nervous, my mouth went totally dry. I couldn't even open my lips, so I just walked away. This was the most embarrassing moment in my life. Afterwards I went to see the professor to apologize.

"Oh, no, you won't get off that easy. Next week you'll have to repeat it, and I am inviting other researchers from various labs to attend." Oh no, I thought. Not that. Hit me in the teeth with a hammer, but don't make me repeat this fiasco. The following week, all I prepared was Beadle and Tatum. Then the time came when I had to give the presentation in front of a room of researchers.

This time I was better prepared, and at the end, all the professor said was, "That will do." Like in the movie *Babe*, when the baby pig saves the day and the farmer tells Babe, "That will do, pig. That will do." So I was like a pig doing an acceptable performance.

So one of my students asked me, "Mr. Rue, now in retrospect, would you still have done it anyway. I mean it was *Star Wars*."

I didn't have to think it over . My answer was a very clear…NO WAY!

Many years later, as a teacher, I recommend to my students, don't procrastinate. And if you do procrastinate and you are not prepared, come clean and just say you aren't prepared. Don't wing it. Accept the consequences, but don't try to trick your audience because you'll only be fooling yourself.

Technologist to Teacher

In 1980 I presented my thesis on The Effect of Starvation on the Development of the Drosophila Melanogaster, and with that, I completed eight years of undergraduate work in Molecular Biology and graduate work in Developmental Genetics. That same summer, I was offered a job by the company I worked for in the summer teaching English. They wanted me to accept a position as director of a summer student exchange program positioned in New York. At first it was exciting and prestigious, but something started happening to me. I was keeping awake at night, thinking, what am I doing? After all the hard work, difficulties, and challenges I went through at the Spanish University getting my degree in Biology, I was now doing a job which had nothing to do with science. So after two years, I resigned from my position as director of the summer program in spite of being happy there. But I wasn't truly satisfied, so I applied to a program to get my license as a Medical Technologist. By the end of the year, I was certified in Hematology, Clinical Chemistry, Parasitology, Endocrinology, and Bacteriology.

During my training, I had an incident occur, which now I find humorous but was not so when it happened. I was stationed in Urinalysis one day when I was approached by Carmen, an elderly lady from "separation" the unit dedicated to separating the samples and delivering to the proper destination.

I was seated doing tests on urine samples when Carmen asked me, "Joe, I got this sample, but it doesn't have a number." Since I was sitting below the height where Carmen was holding her sample, I saw the label was actually placed on the bottom of the tube instead of on the side. I told her the number was on the bottom. Then the unexpected happened. Carmen turned over the tube to see the number, but she hadn't covered the tube, allowing half the content to fall on my back. I quickly caught her hand with the urine and saved the sample, so the patient wouldn't have to return to give us another sample. I could feel the urine flowing down my back under my lab coat. Carmen started apologizing and crying.

Then the supervisor came in the room, shouting, "What's going on here?" Poor Carmen was besides herself. But then a real unexpected turn of events happened. Carmen explained to the supervisor what happened. "I came to Joe to ask about the number, and he told me it was on the bottom, and I turned the tube over to see it, and it came out because I didn't cap it." The strangest thing of this story was that after we saved the original sample, Carmen didn't recap it. And when she explained what happened to the supervisor, she repeated EVERYTHING as it originally occurred, once again pouring the urine on me again. This time it hit me right in the face. I just sat there as the urine got into my eyes and drops fell off my nose. I just sat there at my station incredulous and told the supervisor I was going to wash up in the bathroom. I can now laugh how this was the first and only time I was a recipient of a golden shower.

After a year when I was assigned the night shift, I found my mornings free. In my past, I truly loved my experience when teaching, so I went to Hunter College to get my New York State teaching certificate. Once I got my teaching certificate, I resigned from the lab and I worked one year at St. John's Prep. It was a marvelous experience. At the end of my first year as a teacher, the teachers went on strike, and the majority of the teachers were axed putting an end to my year teaching at

St. John's Prep. I was blessed that there was an opening for a science teacher at Fordham Prep. I, too, loved teaching at Fordham, in fact I loved both places, which fueled my love of teaching. Then Rye Country Day School came next, which you will read about in the chapter called Lino's Sub.

I Hate You

One of the strangest encounters I ever had with a student happened in my first year as a teacher at St. John's Prep. The school was an excellent institution, and the kids were great. They were polite and respectful for the most part. Then I had a strange interaction with one of the boys in homeroom. I was getting a list of students who were going to come on a school trip to Great Adventures Amusement Park. When I reached this boy in question (We'll call him John, but that wasn't really his name), his reaction was so strange to me. I asked him if he was coming on the trip.

He asked me, "Are you going, Mr. Rue?" I told him yes. Then he said, "Well then I am not going because I hate you." My initial reaction was to laugh because I believed this to be a joke. But as I watched him depart, I noticed that he wasn't laughing. Could this be real? We don't usually think about this, but the word hate is a very powerful word. That night I had difficulty sleeping. The next morning, the first thing I did was to ask him about his statement.

"John, I have to know if you meant what you said to me yesterday."

"No, Mr. Rue, I didn't mean it, I am going on the trip." A wave of relief came over me, but then he added, "I didn't mean what I said about the trip, but I did mean what I said about you." I was shocked.

"Why?"

"I can't tell you because I could get kicked out of school."

"I promise that I will not share what you tell me with anyone, but I need to know why you hate me. Did I do anything to get you to be upset with me?"

"No, but I can't tell you."

"Please, John, you have to tell me." He paused a moment and finally agreed.

"Alright, I hate you because…I hate your face. When I see it, I wish I could smack your face." I was in a state of shock hearing this. We paused for a while, then he asked, "Am I going to get kicked out of school because of this?"

"No, John, I gave you my word that I wouldn't get you in trouble."

He then said, "Can I ask you something? Now what do you think of me?"

"Well, John, I think you are a great kid, but I think you have a horrible taste in faces." He smiled. "I don't know why you hate my face so much, but a bit of advice. Don't waste your energy hating somebody because of their face. They can't change it nor should they try. Try being more accepting of others."

"Is that all?" he wondered.

"Yes, that is all." I don't know if this helped him, but at least he was more amiable in homeroom. This happened in my first year being a young teacher. In today's world, I would have sought help from a professional guidance counselor to help this young man with his issues.

San Fermin

In 1984 I was reading some Hemingway, *Fiesta*. In this novel, Hemingway wrote about the running of the bulls in Pamplona. I thought that this had to be a real rush, no pun intended. Then one day, I was proctoring a test at St. John's Prep and I noticed that the homeroom teacher had a quotation by Jack London hanging on the wall.

It went, "I would rather be ashes than dust. I would rather my spark should burn out in a brilliant blaze than it should be stifled in dry rot. I would rather be a superb meteor, every atom of me in a magnificent glow than a sleepy and permanent planet. Man's chief purpose is to live, not to exist. I shall not waste my days trying to prolong them. I shall use my time." It was right then and there that I decided that I wanted to be ashes, not dust. I wanted to try something exciting. I wanted to live, not just exist…I wanted to run the bulls in Pamplona! So I started planning my great adventure. First I studied what to do if a bull reversed direction and started to run after me. I am a biped, and the bull is a quadruped. It is faster than me, but it cannot maneuver as well. So I would need to….zig zag. Next, what should I do if I fall or get tossed to the ground…play dead. Finally, move out of the way if the bull is behind you. I was ready, although I didn't think I would get that close to them. I wanted to experience what it was like without putting myself in danger. The first morning of the run, I made an illegal entry and was ushered out by the mozos in charge, so I watched the bulls pass from the safety of the barricades. But then it happened. A bull gored a runner, and he went down. He obviously didn't do his homework and he didn't know the rules as I did. He started crawling away when he should have played dead. The bulls saw him, returned to him, and took him to the wall with their horns and proceeded to open him up. His intestines were hanging out and he had the most incredible expression on his face as if he were saying, "My guts are out and I'm going to die." Luckily the emergency crew was close by and immediately took him to the hospital and saved him. He was an American Marine from Malta and he survived.

The next day, he was interviewed at the hospital and he said that was an awesome experience, "I can't wait to come back next year." It was an eye-opener for me, but it still didn't sway me from wanting to run. So the next morning, I got up early and walked to the start of the route. On the way there, I saw a young kid who was quite nervous.

He asked me, "Mister, are you going to the Encierro, the running of the bulls?"

"Yeah, I am," I replied.

"Will you run with me?" he asked. "I'm very nervous."

"Sure, kid. Where do you want to run? In front of the bulls, or do you want to let them pass and run behind the bulls?"

He replied, "Between the bulls." Now there are six bulls and six harmless steers. The bulls are the dangerous ones, especially if they get separated from the group. People run in front of the bulls, but every now and then there are some that run in between the bulls.

"Do you mean in between the bulls?" I asked him.

"You and I are going to run in between the bulls." I patted the kid on his back and said good luck and I took off. I had no intention of being a hero or a suicidal runner. I went to the corral where the bulls were being kept and I made a legal entry to the running route. Moments before starting, we saluted the statue of San Fermin and offered him a short song. We saluted him with a rolled-up newspaper in our hand. I then started to make my way to the front of the route. They shot off two rockets to indicate the bulls were on their way. I ran so far ahead that when I reached the bullfighting ring, everybody booed me. I was like the day's coward. I didn't care, I just wanted to see what it felt like. Finally the bulls arrived to the ring and were placed in the stables. Well that was fun, I thought, and I started heading back to the entrance where the bulls had just passed through. Then it happened. One bull was left behind. This was the sixth bull and the most dangerous since he was separated from the pack. I should have counted them. Before I could realize it, there it was, some seven meters in front of me. It was gigantic with big horns resembling a demon. It saw me and came right after me, but I remembered the tips I had read about running the bulls. I started to run. At first it followed, but I zigzagged, making it hard for the bull to catch me. It did not continue after me. Soon there were many people jumping in between me and the bull taking the opportunity to bullfight this deadly creature. In the main plaza of Pamplona, Plaza Castilla, it was tradition to hang some pictures of the bravest moments of the day. Once I was back in Madrid, I received a call from Miguel when he told me there was one of me with the bull right at my heels. Little did they know I was not brave; I was stupid. On my way back to the apartment where I was staying, I stopped at a phone booth and I called my family (remember this was before cell phones).

My sister got on the phone and immediately asked me, "Did you do it already?"

"But I told you I wasn't going to run the bulls," and she replied, "I know you, Joey; you ran the bulls."

"Yeah, I did, but all was well." The truth is you put yourself in danger and it is really not worth it. I thought I was going to be the first runner to die of a heart attack. I was so frightened. Years later my friend Miguel asked me if I wanted to run again, but I had done it and I had satisfied my curiosity. No more. From now on, it would be a spectator sport for me and I could be found behind the barriers watching thousands of runners go by.

Lino's Sub

It was 1985, and I was home when I received a phone call from an ex-colleague of mine from St. John's Prep, Lino Brocco.

"What's up, Lino?" After a few pleasantries, he asked me a question.

"Joe, I have an appointment to see a school in Westchester tomorrow, but I can't make it, so I was wondering whether you would like to go in my place."

"Thanks for thinking of me, but I'm teaching now at Fordham Prep and I like it there, so I'm not looking for another school."

"That's OK, Joe. You should go to see what else is out there, and if anything, you get a free lunch." Since I was off the next day and didn't have any plans, I told him I would go.

So I went to the admissions office and asked, "Is this Rye Country Club School?" The secretaries laughed and corrected me saying It's Rye Country Day School, but she sent me to see the Science Department chair Bruce Carlsten.

When I arrived, he said, "Mr. Brocco, I was looking forward to meeting you," to which I replied, "I'm not Lino Brocco. I'm Joe Rue."

He looked through his papers and said, "I don't seem to have your information here."

"That's right because I'm taking his place."

He said, "This is most curious, are you at least a biology teacher?"

"Yes, I am."

So I went through all the steps that a prospective candidate goes through, and at the end of the day, I had an interview with the principal of the school, and he asked, "Joe, can I ask you a personal question. Why are you not happy at Fordham Prep?"

"I am," I replied.

"Well then why do you want to leave?"

"I don't," I replied.

"Well what are you doing here?" I told him my friend Leno Brocco couldn't make it, so I took his place. "I have never heard of anything like this. Well there's one question left. Everybody has spoken very positively of you, and I want to ask is there any possibility of getting you to come to our school?"

I sat there for a moment thinking and I said, "Yeah, there is a possibility."

I though it over, and the rest is history.

One of the teachers I met that day was Dennis Sullivan. I asked him how many years had he been teaching at RCDS? Nine years, he replied. I thought to myself, who stays nine years in the same place? Something must be wrong with him. And now I understand because I have been thirty-seven years at RCDS and it is a great institution and I loved every year teaching there.

Pet Peeves

In class I often tell the students to keep their eyes on the teacher and the front board. It reminds me of another pet peeve. Have you ever noticed in movies and TV shows how the drivers often look at their passengers, taking their eyes off the road? When they're not looking at the road for long periods of time, how do they not get into an accident? In a similar fashion, I tell the students to pay attention "to the road."

Over the course of the years, I have acquired a few pet peeves. These are things that you usually hear and disagree with what they are or how they are pronounced. For example one of the pet peeves that irritates me is the way people say the word *nuclear*. From President Bush to Jack Bauer in the series *24*, people erroneously say NUCULAR instead of NUCLEAR. "We have to prevent a *nucular* explosion."

Another pet peeve is the misuse of the words *hypothesis* and *theory*. A hypothesis is a proposed solution to a problem. For example the cells of the wings of a starving fly should be smaller than the cells of a control well-fed fly. A theory is the best-established explanation based on facts, such as the cell theory, tells us that all living things are made of cells based on universal observations. Well, in police shows, you constantly hear a detective say, *"I have a theory"* when he should be saying *"I have a hypothesis."*

Another pet peeve is the pronunciation of words with a W instead of *wyte* like *whuite*.

Another pet peeve is more of an expectation of civility. When we are having a conversation, I really dislike people who interrupt while you are speaking. They should wait their turn or wait for you to stop speaking. This is more an example of common courtesy and respect.

Have you ever been in a situation where you are talking and you say something, but everyone ignores your comment? Little while later, you repeat your comment and everybody once again ignores it. Finally somebody else repeats your comment and everyone acknowledges it. What am I….chopped liver? I jokingly say that when I am ignored, "I feel like a mushroom. In the dark and surrounded by manure."

The Pick Pocket

I was walking in Greenwich Village with my friends Joe and Sissy. We were crossing 6th Avenue when I noticed that Sissy's bag was open. I asked her if she was missing something, and she replied that her wallet must've fallen out. I looked at an individual nicely dressed walking right behind her. When he saw me checking him out, he suddenly broke into a run. I instinctively started running after him. He went down into the subway and jumped the turnstiles to enter. I illogically searched through my pockets for a token, inserted the token, and continued the chase. At this point, he exited the subway, and I was on the other side of the avenue. He continued running. I ran across the avenue doing what they do in cop series, raising my arms and stopping the ongoing traffic. He was gaining distance, and I was losing him when I heard a voice asking if I was OK.

Out of the corner of my eye, I saw a police uniform and I shouted, "I've been robbed." Like a sprinter in an Olympic race, this officer took up the chase and passed me, running after the thief. By this time, I had fallen behind and I was only able to continue in the right direction by seeing all the passerby's looking at the chase. I reached a short street where the officer was waiting.

He told me, "He's somewhere down this street. Go around the block, and we will lock him in." By the time I got to the end of the street by going around the block, there were multiple policemen and three squad cars. I kept aside while the police closed in, making a pincer move. Then to my surprise, they found the robber hiding down a stairwell. Even more surprising, Sissy's wallet was on the floor where he had tossed it. The robber was arrested, and they took me to the police station. As I entered, various policemen clapped as I went by.

One approached me and said, "You did a good job, but what you did was very dangerous. He could have been armed. What were you planning to do?" Well the truth is I just wanted the wallet back. I wasn't planning on fighting him. In my naivety, I was just going to ask him nicely. Besides, he was bigger than me, and I wouldn't fare well in a fight. Afterwards all calmed down, and they took my statement. The officer thought it was humorous that during a chase, I stopped to find a token instead of jumping the turnstile. They mentioned that they were after this individual for some time. When we finished, I went home.

There is a funny follow up to this story. My friends have heard me tell it multiple times, but one day a friend of mine told it, but he inserted himself in the tale. In his story, he was right next to me during the chase. He insisted that he was there. I had no problem with this new version, but it wasn't what really happened. I started doubting and I checked with Sissy, but she confirmed that it was just her, Joe, and me. As I mentioned in the introduction, stories can change and evolve with time after being told.

Dr. Seuss

There were two sermons I heard that especially left a mark on me. The first was given by a young priest. He spoke of how children all over the world were dying of hunger. Then he said most people don't give a shit. And he concluded by saying that the sad thing is that most people are offended by him saying "shit" in his sermon than by the fact that millions of children are dying of hunger. This hit home, and I realized that we don't always prioritize what is really important.

The second sermon I'm referring to today is one a priest said about Dr. Seuss. He was invited to speak at a prestigious university to give the commencement speech. They were expecting him to talk for an hour more or less. Dr. Seuss got up and said the following:

My Uncle Terwillinger on the art of eating popovers. My uncle ordered popovers from the restaurant's bill of fare. And when they were served, he regarded them with a penetrating stare…Then he spoke great words of wisdom – as he sat there on that chair. 'To eat these things,' said my uncle, 'you must exercise great care. You swallow down what's solid. But you must spit out the air!'

He then proceeded to sit down, some say…to the dismay of the leadership of the school. But this might be part of the legend of this tale since the chances were that they in reality knew what he would say. Whether they knew it or not, that doesn't change the great lesson Dr.

Seuss was teaching the students....and the importance of brevity. I usually start the year in Biology with this story and I ask my students, what was the importance of what he was saying?

This important lesson can help you in this course but also in your career as a student in high school and college. Learn what is solid and throw away the fluff.

Subway Brawl

Living in New York, I would often get visitors from other parts of the world. One year I had two friends visiting from Germany. One night Marion, Annetta and I went out with a friend of mine, Jim, to a Brazilian dance hall called SOB (Sounds of Brazil). We danced till 2 A.M. and then headed back home. We decided to take the subway back to Queens. As we entered the subway car, we encountered a group of some twelve young men in their twenties who had been out drinking. When the subway started to move, one of the young men came over to Annetta and jumped on her. He rolled on top of her, scaring the daylights out of her. I grabbed this individual from behind and separated him from Annetta.

"Woah, fella, you had too much to drink. Calm down," I said. The next thing I knew, the other eleven drunks jumped me, forming a full-fledged brawl. There were too many of them. They grabbed my head, they grabbed my arms, my legs, and moved me like a ragdoll. They threw Jim between the cars (the train was stopped by this point), and most riders had evacuated the train. Then they threw me on the platform. All I could think about was that my two German friends were alone in the car with the drunks. Anything could happen to them. They made a wall at the entrance of the subway car to stop me from reentering. I jumped high over the human wall, falling to the floor within the subway car. The next thing I knew, I was on the floor while the drunks were kicking me. To be honest, since there were so many, they were kicking themselves as much as me. I finally got up and started pushing them away. At this point, one of the twelve extended his hand and said that's enough, let's finish this. I didn't trust them. Sure enough, when he got in arm's length from me, he kicked so high that if he would have connected, he would have broken my jaw. But my reflexes from fencing helped me quickly retreat and hold his leg. At this point, I had the option of punching him between the legs, but I didn't. I really wanted to stop him, but I had no intention of hurting anyone. Not even these idiots. I just pushed him down. Finally a young police rookie arrived.

I said to her, "Officer, arrest these guys."

She asked, "Are you pressing charges?"

The one who had tried to kick me came close to me and said in a little voice, "If you say anything to her, if you press charges, we will hunt you down and kill you."

I immediately said to the police officer, "I press charges, especially for this one." He then raised his fist in an attempt to punch me. I said to him go ahead, punch me and the police officer will shoot you. So although this wouldn't have happened, it was enough to stop him from further aggression. She was able to detain and cuff two of the twelve, but that was OK with me.

At the station, the violent one quickly said, "I want to press charges against this man. He attacked us." I was in a state of shock. Could this actually happen? The police man looked at my face, which was swollen, and then looked at the drunkard's fists, which were red which indicated that he was using them to hit something or better said someone. Me.

The police officer after observing this said, "I don't think so."

At this point, the young man spit in the officer's face, and he said, "You are a Mickey Mouse cop. We'll be out soon."

"Maybe, but we'll see." The officer kept his cool, took our statements, but obviously he was upset. After giving our statement and answering all their questions, we were ready to leave. We grabbed a subway back home.

Marion was very impressed and said, "This was like a TV episode of Kojak." Annetta was still in shock. Jim's wrist was sore from when they threw him between the cars, but he was alright. All in all, a very exciting night in the Big Apple.

Chitin

When we cover the topic of polysaccharides when studying carbo-
hydrates, we give examples. There are polysaccharides of storage (for
energy) and polysaccharides of structure. In plants a polysaccharide of
storage is starch, and in animals, a polysaccharide of storage is glycogen
found in the liver. In plants a polysaccharide of structure is cellulose,
while in animals a polysaccharide of structure is chitin. I find it humorous that students often miss pronounce this word like shit-in. Chitin
(pronounced like kyte-in) would be found in the exoskeleton of arthro-
pods, such as insects. At this point, I usually ask if anyone has ever eaten
chitin? Most say no; however, the chances are that we have eaten insects
in our lives. When we eat a salad, what appears as little specs of pepper
can often be the bodies of small insects. So I tell them a story which
happened to me some years back. I was coming home from work and I
stopped to get some takeout food. It was beef and broccoli. When I got
home, I turned on the TV, and they were showing the movie *Jaws*. I
was quickly engulfed in the story while eating my food straight from
the carton, honestly not paying much attention to my food. My eyes
were glued on the TV, but then I noticed I ate a piece of beef that was
very crunchy outside and juicy inside. It was delicious. I continued eating while watching the movie and I got another piece of beef crunchy
on the outside and juicy on the inside. This was rapidly becoming my

favorite takeout place. Then the commercial aired, and I observed my food more carefully. In it were pieces of beef and pieces of broccoli and also…water bugs. Giant roaches cooked with the other food. I realized the juicy crunchy pieces of beef were roaches. I have eaten insects before, but I was always aware of their presence. Here they were surprises. Psychologically I kept feeling them moving in my stomach, but I know this was not the case since they were fried, chewed, and digested. I called a friend of mine who worked at the Department of Health and I reported the restaurant. He told me that this was not the first complaint and eventually they closed down the establishment. The motto of this story is watch what you are eating for you might get a surprise.

Popcorn

Anyone who knows me knows that I love movies. I'm a real movie buff and film collector, owning over 3,000 DVD and Blu Rays. But still there is nothing like going to the movies with a friend, getting a soda and a bucket of popcorn and munching away during the film. A close buddy of mine didn't take the popcorn route as I did. Instead he would always get a box of Raisinets and some Twizzlers. I would tell him that those snacks had a lot of sugar and he should eat popcorn instead. Although there is one thing that was surprising me. I seem to be gaining weight with my usual snacks. It wasn't until I read an article talking about the caloric value of popcorn at the movies. It claimed that one bucket of popcorn with butter and a large soda would be equal to the following:

- Two eggs, bacon, coffee and orange juice in the morning.
- A McDonald Big Mac, fries, a soda, and an apple pie for lunch.
- A steak, a baked potato, a glass of wine and a yogurt for dessert for dinner

This blew my mind. Back then the popcorn was prepared with coconut oil, which was less healthy than vegetable oil, but it was very delicious. Nevertheless, even today with theaters that don't use coconut oil, it is still very high in calories. Popcorn is considered a healthy snack if you air pop it, not using oil and if you don't overdo it.

A creepy fact, the FDA allows a small percentage of rat poop and roach pieces in your movie popcorn. And though it is a small percentage, how would you feel if you got the rat pellet in your popcorn?

Champagne

One of the topics we cover every year in Biology is Aerobic Cellular Respiration. As a follow-up, we explain Anaerobic Cellular Respiration. This process starts with glucose (for example a sugar found in grape juice) and undergoes glycolysis through a series of some ten steps, producing alcohol and carbon dioxide. This is what we know as fermentation. And when this topic is explained, inevitably the story of Dom Perignon comes up. The myth is that Dom Perignon was a blind Benedictine monk living in an abbey in the 1600s in the Champagne region of France. One can hear many myths about this man, including he was the discoverer of champagne and of corks for the champagne bottles. The story I heard was that this blind monk accidentally sealed white wine in such a way that the gas would not leave. The story continued that the monks brought this wine to King Louis XIV. When they poured the wine and the monks saw the bubbles, they panicked. What would the king say, but when the king tried this new wine, he loved it, making it one of the most popular wines in the region.

In reality most of this myth is just that, a false description of the story of Dom Perignon. Around 1990 I attended a forensic science conference where one of the talks was about Dom Perignon. The presenters had researched his journals and came to the conclusion that he was definitely not blind and furthermore the production of champagne was not a quirk but was well studied. In fact Dom Perignon came up with his version of champagne, contributing to our understanding of this refreshing bubbly drink, helping to make it more acceptable. Up to then, for most wineries, the bubbles were a major flaw, not an asset.

Another myth that should be corrected is as follows. It is often said that when Dom Perignon first tried his champagne, he called out to his fellow monks, saying, "Come quickly, I am tasting the stars." This, too, seems to be a fabrication, which didn't appear till centuries later, in the 1880s, in a champagne commercial.

And now that we have a better understanding of champagne, let's open a bottle and toast Dom Perignon.

Footnote: One of the most prestigious wineries, Möet & Chandon, produced their first champagne in 1921, which they named "Dom Pérignon" after this famous scientist and pioneer in the champagne industry.

https://www.luxuryfacts.com › index.php › sections › article › Dom-Perignon——-The-Kings-Entourage
https://www.brightcellars.com › blog › dom-perignon
https://www.epiccellars.com › post › 5-myths-about-dom-pérignon-debunked
https://fizzicality.co.uk › 2017 › 04 › 21 › first-blog-post

Happy Halloween

When I started teaching at Rye Country Day School in 1985, one of the traditions was that most students and teachers would dress up for Halloween. Over the years, the tradition became less, although a handful of teachers would still dress up. In my thirty-seven years teaching there, I dressed up with a different costume every year. Even in the pandemic, I dressed up as Batman on Zoom. Common belief is that I love dressing up, but the fact is I did it more to maintain a lost tradition. So over close to four decades, I have been a variety of characters, never repeating. My favorites were Frodo, Sherlock Holmes, Dracula, Darth Vader, a zombie, the Phantom of the Opera, Sam Adams, Zorro, a pirate, Clark Kent, and a Plague Doctor among many more. One of my first costume was showing up in my fencing whites. One of my students, Andrew Gums, asked me if I have ever fenced. I then found that he was a fencer. That encounter led us to begin a fencing team at RCDS.

However, my all-time favorite costume was the year I came as the Wolfman. I had a beard and longer hair, so I cut my hair and used actors glue to paste hair all over my face. I darkened my nose and I truly looked like a wolf. Back then there was no Easy Pass, so I had to go through a tollbooth. The attendant saw me and gave a shout. I apologized and reminded him it was Halloween. When I arrived to school, I didn't see anybody dressed up and I panicked for a while, thinking I got the wrong day. But then people started arriving with costumes.

One Senior saw me, came over to me, and said right in my face, "Who the f*** are you?"

I moved right up to him, growled, and said, "I'm Mr. Rue." He apologized, arguing that he didn't realize it was me and he thought I was another student. I asked him, "Is that the way you would approach another student?" He apologized and left. That was my most memorable costume.

Another Halloween moment was when my wife got tickets for a Japanese concert in Carnegie Hall. Since it was Halloween, I asked her if people would be dressed up. She guaranteed me that they would all be dressed up. So I show up as Indiana Jones, complete with the leather jacket, fedora, whip, a black eye, and spider webs all over. When I arrived to my surprise, most guests were Japanese and everyone was dressed up…to the nines with evening wear. I commented to my wife that she said everyone would be dressed up, and she replied they were dressed up. I was so embarrassed, wanting to hide being the only person in a costume. To make matters worse, Japanese television was waiting outside, interviewing the concert goers. The second they saw me, they ran over to interview me. I assured them that that wasn't my normal dress, but I explained Halloween to the Japanese audience. My wife told me that that segment aired in Tokyo and her family saw me. What a way to make an impression.

Happy Halloween!

BI-ART-LOGY

In 1996 I was teaching a class when I mentioned 50 percent of a substance dissolved and I noticed that one of my students drew a happy face, half smiling and half dissolved. Her name was Sayaka Ogata and she had just recently come to the US from Japan. After noticing her drawing, I asked her if she could see me after class. The poor girl was so nervous, thinking I was going to reprimand her for her drawing. The fact was that she had laced her notes with creative drawings while still recording all the information.

"Mr. Rue, I'm so sorry for drawing in my notebook. It won't happen again!" she said.

"On the contrary, I want you to draw," I said. "I'd like you to help me," I replied. She just stood there with a confused expression on her face.

"I don't understand. It might be a language barrier, but it sounds like you are asking me to help you, but you are the teacher and I am just the student," she replied. "How could I help you?"

"Well, you see, the kids are having a hard time visualizing photosynthesis, and I think your drawings could help them," I said.

"So I'm not in trouble?" she asked. And that was the start of what came to be called BI-ART-LOGY. We decided to cartoon all the topics in the honors biology curriculum. On November 1st, 1999, Sayaka and

I presented at the STANYS Conference, Bi-ART-LOGY: A Work in Progress. It was a big hit among the teachers who saw the presentation. Sayaka was the star of the show. There were many requests for the finished product, but alas, that was not meant to be at that point. Sayaka went off to college, and the book was put on hold.

The second student involved with BI-ART-LOGY was Matthew Jacobson, who contributed drawings starting in 2000. However, we couldn't advance much, and the book was relegated to gaining spider webs in my closet.

Then in 2009, I came across a third artistically talented student who was willing to get involved with the project, Cynthia Luo. We worked hard on completing the book, but once again, we fell short.

And finally, in 2015, the fourth and final student to be involved with this book came along and added the impetus to complete these twenty-two-year long projects. His name was Jialin Yang and he was as talented and motivated as the previous three artistic students. We presented once more the now completed book at the 2018 STANYS Science Conference with Jialin in person and Sayaka on Zoom.

Much of the above text is borrowed from the introduction of the graphic arts book, BI-ART-LOGY, and I hope anyone interested in biology will have the opportunity to check out this artistic journey through the different topics in biology.

The Siblings

The students at RCDS have always been great in so many ways. From small details like thanking me at the end of class, to stepping up to do something above and beyond. An example of this happened years ago. We had a lobster tank in our classroom, but regretfully our lobster died. It was a sealed tank, and a layer of scum developed from the decomposed lobster. So one day we had a test, and while I was proctoring, I decided to clean out the tank. This was a bad decision. I removed the top lid, and immediately a wave of putrefaction assaulted my nose. My gosh, it was appalling. Within seconds it permeated the room, and the students started gagging and making a massive exodus from the room, leaving the test behind.

I called out, "Can someone stay to help me clean out the tank?" Too late, they were gone. Honestly I don't blame them. The smell was so horrendous that I wanted to run out. But then the unexpected occurred. One of my students slowly returned.

Sean said, "We can do this, Mr. Rue." And together we cleaned out this rotting mess. Sean went on to become a close friend and captain of the fencing team. In fact I became very close to the whole family, Sean, Brian, Bridget, their delightful sister, Conor and their dad, David, and Mom, Maureen. His brother, Brian, also became captain of the fencing team. One incident that stands out was at the finals of the ISFL (Independent School Fencing League). Brian won his bout, placing us as the gold medal winners. Brian was already changing in the locker room when the directors caught a mistake that we actually tied for first place with Chapin/Misc. We sent a fencer to get Brian because we had to redo the last bout to determine the winner. The doors leading from the lockers finally opened, and the silhouette of a fencer appeared with a strong light behind him. It was Brian. It looked like a scene out of an adventure film. In spite of all the pressure, he refenced the last bout and he won again. The third brother Conor, who I knew since he was a little boy, also became the captain of the fencing team. It was around that time when I had a friend whose son was going through a difficult time. He was extremely shy and wouldn't talk to people. But he liked swashbuckler movies. So I asked Conor for a favor. Let's go fully equipped to this young boy's garage and fence. Conor was like a miracle worker having the young boy talk, interact, and fence. It was a delight to watch.

Sean, Brian, Conor, and their sister Bridget shared one thing in common. They all had big hearts and had giving personalities. I became close friends with the four siblings. The three boys went on to be Captains of the fencing team, proving to be outstanding fencers leading three generations of RCDS fencers to victorious and successful seasons. Bridget, though not a fencer, was a most important member of these siblings being altruistic and caring. These young students were a reflection of the type of caring students I encountered at RCDS.

Telomeres

I formed and taught a most interesting elective called Science and Society. This course didn't have a set curriculum nor a textbook. Each student picked a topic in science that was affecting society, and after spending a semester honing their skills, they became semi-experts in their topic. Each student would research their topic and share information with the class. By the end of the elective, each student would teach a whole class on their topic. They selected genetic engineering, cloning, spider webbing, space travel, viral epidemics, and on and on. One of my students selected the topic of human aging. Connected to this topic was the shortening of telomeres on the chromosomes. Humans have forty-six chromosomes in each and every somatic (body) cell, except for gamete (sex) cells, which have twenty-three. On the somatic cells, the chromosomes have tips called telomeres. Every time a cell divides and copies itself (replicates), the tips have difficulties copying themselves, and the telomeres get shorter. As the telomeres get shorter, the organism ages. The world expert on telomere studies is an American scientist, Bill Andrews. My student followed Dr. Andrew's experiments and ideas.

One day, talking with his mom, he said, "Wouldn't it be wonderful if Dr. Andrews could come talk to our class at RCDS?"

His mom asked, "Why don't you invite him?"

"Mom, he is a world figure and a very important scientist who would not have time to come to a high school class. It would be like inviting Robert De Niro to a high school acting class. He would be too busy."

"Well, if you don't ask him, he'll never come, so give it a try." He took that to heart and tracked down a number for Dr. Andrews. After talking with secretaries and other representatives of Dr. Andrews, he eventually contacted him. He invited him to our class and he accepted. He was giving a lecture in California, but he said he would Skype our class. My students and the AP bio students anxiously filled the classroom, looking forward to our talk with Dr. Andrews. It was amazing. He was so personable, knowledgeable, and generous with his time that he impressed us all. He was respectful and friendly, never condescending to any of the high school students. I felt like his talk was so informative, and it was truly a worthwhile encounter.

Then after some thirty minutes or so, we could hear someone knocking at his door, saying, "Doctor, the guests are waiting for you."

He replied, "Tell them I will be right there." He apologized that he had to leave, but just before leaving, he said that there was a girl in the back of the classroom who had a question and he said he would answer one more question. This was reflective of his respect for the young minds and future scientists. It was truly a memorable class for all. And another very important lesson was learned, you must be willing to put yourself out there and do what might originally seem impossible.

Edible Biology

Early on in my teaching career, one day I was teaching taxonomy, and a student asked me, "Why do we need to learn these names and classifications (taxonomy) if we never will encounter them, I mean I won't meet up with an octopus." That night I mulled over that student's question. Where would we encounter these? Of course on our dinner plates.

So the next day I prepared my edible taxonomy test. I cooked up a paella with rice, peas, shrimp, mussels, octopus, carrots, chicken, peppers, mushrooms, onions, seaweed, and spices (saffron). As the students entered the classroom, they encountered a makeshift restaurant with plates, glasses, forks, napkins, and a menu at each desk. The menu was actually the test. They had to answer matching questions as the appetizers. Then the main course was identifying the Kingdom, Phylum, Class, and Order where applicable. Meanwhile, wearing an apron, I went to each student with a cloth over my arm asking red or white and serving them Coke or 7 Up. The students were amazed, and they saw the first-hand connection of taxonomy.

This was the start of my edible bio classes. When we study the Fungus Kingdom, I cooked up Shitashi and Button mushrooms. I add a little garlic and slices of beef jerky. I serve with matzo crackers. This is a favorite of the class.

But the one that impresses the students the most and positively surprises them is the Anticucho. So what is anticucho? Let's go back some twenty-five years when I went to Peru. One night I went to a restaurant and asked the waiter to bring me the specialty of the house. He replied Anticucho. He brought me a shish kabab type dish. It was delicious, but something intrigued me. Coming out of the chunks of meat were these thread-like structures. Have you ever seen a film and you recognize an actor but can't place him/her from another film? Well that was the experience I was having. I recognized these chords but couldn't place them. Chords? Chords? Then it came to me.

I called over the waiter and asked him, "Excuse me, but is this heart?" It was. So that moment became a highlight of my class. When we cover the circulatory system, I bring hearts from a local butcher, and we dissect them in class, seeing the four chambers, the valves, and the chordae tendinae…the chords. After dissecting the hearts, I remove the outer membrane Epicardium and the inner membrane Endocardium, leaving just the pure cardiac muscle, the Myocardium. I take out an electric skillet, add some olive oil, garlic, and a pinch of salt and pepper.

Once a student asked me, "Mr. Rue, is this a clean piece of meat?" It's from within the body. You won't get a cleaner piece of meat. When you eat a steak, it is coming from its rear end. When I serve the students, they are surprised that it is so delicious. "This is better than a sirloin. It has no grizzle, no fat, no nerves. You can even slice it with a fork, it is so tender."

What surprises me is that, other than vegetarians and vegans, most students give it a try…and like it.

Student who had me in previous years come to the classroom and say, "We can smell you cooking up something. Is it heart day? Can we have some?" Sure, why not. Anything to get the kids excited about learning.

English in Spain

It was 1990, and I was hoping to get a summer job to supplement my income. I got a summer job teaching English in a language camp in Madrid. My students were nine and ten-years-old and they were beginners in English. I decided to use the method I employed when my nephew, David, and niece, Crissy, were very young. To force them to speak English at home, I acted as if I didn't understand Spanish, which I am fluent in.

For example I had just returned from New York, and one morning my nephew came to my room and asked, "Uncle Joey, vamos a jugar" (Uncle Joey, let's play). I feigned ignorance of Spanish and forced him to ask in English. He knew a little English, but it was minimal. In this manner, we spent the summer speaking in English. I returned to New York to my teaching job, but I went back to Spain for Christmas. When I arrived, my mom said it's a pity, but David doesn't speak English anymore. We talk to him in English, and he replies in Spanish. So I picked up my luggage and went to the car where David was waiting for me with my dad.

At first he didn't say much at all, then to everyone's surprise, he turned to me and in perfect English said, "When we get home, can we play, Uncle Joey?" My mother and everyone else in the car was shocked to hear David say those words in perfect English.

My mom asked, "David, if we ask you in English for anything, you answer in Spanish. If you know English, why don't you respond in English?" He said that Uncle Joey lives in New York, and they speak English there. You live in Madrid where Spanish is spoken. That was a clear explanation of his logic.

Getting back to my summer job, I decided to use the same method where I told the students I only spoke English and I didn't understand Spanish. In reality I was fluent. They would test me and say in Spanish things like, "Teacher, your nose looks like a potato." I would have to avoid laughing or showing any indication that I understood.

"What is that? Can you please say it in English." They looked at each other, reconfirming the fact that I knew no Spanish.

Another day a child approached me and said, "Joe tengo que ir al bano"

"What?" I inquired.

He repeated, "Joe tengo que ir al bano."

"I'm sorry, what is that?"

He then said, "I bathroom." Sure. It was hard to maintain the ruse, but it was worthwhile. One day I was talking with the other English teachers, and one of my students came running to me and said in English, "Teacher, teacher, Patricia is hyperventilation. I went to help her, she was fine." When I returned, the other teachers asked how did I get them to talk to me in English, even in an emergency situation.

I smiled, "They really believe I don't speak Spanish, so they are forced to speak English."

Teaching English in Spain was a different experience than teaching biology in New York, but both were rewarding.

Barretstown

One day I was approached by a buddy of mine who was my partner teaching English at Spanish summer camps.

"Hey, Joe, I heard of a camp in Ireland for children with cancer and serious illnesses. Why don't we give it a try?" Well I thought about it and came to the conclusion that this could be a great opportunity to help young children who were facing difficulties in life. As it turned out, my friend couldn't make it because an obligation came up with his own children, but I was already committed to the idea. So I signed on for two weeks as a Cara (Counselor) at The Barretstown Gang Camp in County Kildare. The camp grew around a castle, which once belonged to Elizabeth Arden. There was a lake with boats, an area for fishing in the stocked lake, horse stables for riding, an archery range, a rope course, a theater, hiking trails, arts and crafts workshops, and much more. This camp was modelled after Paul Newman's *The Hole In The Wall Camp* in Connecticut, USA. Children from all over Europe arrived to participate in ten-day sessions free of charge. I was blessed to be a counselor there for six summers, and they were life altering experiences. The camp had a medical center, which didn't look like a hospital at all. It was built like Winnie the Pooh's Corner with a very friendly and homey appearance. Before each session, there was a training session for the volunteers. It was a great learning and bonding experience. However, in my first year participating in the program before the children arrived, I started having doubts. Would I be good enough? Would I be strong enough? Could I help the campers? These moments of self-doubt kept me up at night a few days before the campers arrived. Then the day came when the first bus reached our camp. The door opened, and a young girl with a kerchief around her head came off the bus. She saw us, the counselors, waiting, and the most beautiful smile I have ever seen just illuminated her face filling me with a warmth and loving feeling. It was like the sun breaking through the clouds, brightening the day. From that moment on, I realized I wasn't working with patients, I was working with children who happened to have particular conditions. We developed friendships, played, laughed, and enjoyed ourselves. We were all like children singing by the campfires, making smores, participating in fun activities. There were two Australian Caras who had just returned from the running of the bulls in Pamplona, Spain. They would tell us stories of the running of the bulls. Then it occurred to me, why not organize the running of the bulls right here in Barretstown? We set aside sections for spectators, gave the runners red kerchiefs and rolled up newspapers to lead on the bulls, and we had three bulls in the stables. The bulls were actually three Caras dressed as bulls with head dresses with paper horns. A whistle indicated the start of the race, and the three bulls chased after the runners. We ran through the whole camp and had a joyous time. That was one of the many things I loved about the camp. Any idea wasn't crazy enough as long as it sparked the campers' fantasies and as long as it was safe for all. The recurrent image from my experience at the camp was that of happy smiling children.

China

I've been fascinated with the Chinese culture for the longest time, and what got me so interested? Chinese movies. I followed the career of Andy Lao, Zhang ZiYi, Gong Li, Chow Yung Fat, Jackie Chan, and Ekin Cheng. One day there was a booth set up in my school's main corridor. It described a program taking American students to China for the summer. I approached and asked some questions, then asked if they were accepting adults to work as teachers in this program? The young representative replied that they had been searching for an American chaperone to act as director of the program. After months of interviews, they were down to the last three. She then asked me why I was interested in China. I laughed and said actually it was because of Chinese movies. She then asked me to name one of my favorite movies. I had just recently seen one with Ekin Cheng called *A Man Called Hero*. She got excited saying that she loved that movie and asked me to name another. *The Road Home* directed by Zhang Zimou. She said that was another one of her favorite movies.

"We need someone like you," she said. That afternoon I received a call from a director of the company saying that after months of searching, their representative was so impressed with me, and they wanted to interview me.

"You have gone to the top of our list. You will have a great experience staying in a five-star hotel, you will have a chauffeur and a reception in the embassy." I would be working with the American students in our program. That was all exciting, but it wasn't what I was looking for. I did my research and found another program where I would be in a rural school in a small village an hour north of XiAn working with Chinese students. Their director told me I'd be staying in very humble boarding conditions. That is OK, I replied. He repeated that I would be in a very humble room. I mean how bad could it be? As it turned out, the room was fine. And I wasn't going there for the housing, I was going to work with local students. So I opted for the Chinese program where I would work with Chinese children.

There were another three American English teachers working in this summer program an hour from XiAn by bus. Our first obligation was to test the students' level, so we could place them in the proper class. I found their English to be quite excellent. Then one student came in, and he was literally shaking.

"Are you OK?" I asked him.

"I am very afraid," he replied.

"Are you afraid of the entrance test?"

"No," he replied.

"Are you afraid of our interview?"

"No," he replied again.

"So what are you afraid of?"

"I'm afraid of you."

"I don't understand. Why are you afraid of me?"

"I have never met a foreigner…a non-Chinese, and I don't know how I should behave with you." I smiled and tried to put him at ease.

"You'll be OK. you have nothing to worry about. Together we will overcome any difficulties."

So once we completed our interviews, the English teachers decided to walk down to the local bar and have a beer to celebrate our first night in XiAn. We stopped at a very humble establishment and we sat outside in folding chairs. Some fifteen minutes after sitting there, a police officer came by and asked if he could sit down. I wondered what he wanted. Were they keeping tabs on us? The policeman then proceeded to ask questions about the NBA. His English was quite good. Honestly I wasn't the person to speak to about basketball. I knew as much about the NBA as I know about Mars.

But we maintained a very pleasant conversation, and then at some point he said, "I don't want to bother you anymore. Thank you," and he left. He was very friendly, and we enjoyed his visit. After an hour past, a young woman who spoke some English approached us with a child, probably seven-years-old, and asked if it would be OK if the child sang a welcome song for us. Her name was Xiao Hui, and she was a real doll. She had a beautiful voice and her song was so charming, though we didn't understand the words. When she finished, they thanked us for allowing them to welcome us. In fact we were the ones who were grateful. This mother and her child did not want anything from us, they were just happy to be able to welcome us to their small village. This was a lovely start to our stay in China.

Dumplings

So one afternoon, the three English teachers decided to make our way to XiAn and explore the city. From walking around the city walls to checking out the market place, this was a magical place. I thought it was a curious thing that babies would freak out when they saw me close up. They were not accustomed to seeing a person with light eyes. My eyes are light hazel colored and even look bluish at times…enough to startle these young babies. The residents of XiAn were delightful, often asking to have pictures taken of them and me. I truly felt like a celebrity leaving me, wondering how many pictures of me are hanging in Chinese houses.

One of my favorite events happened in the main plaza of XiAn, when the three of us decided to stop and have dinner. Before ordering I checked to see if I had enough money. As it turns out, I was way short, so I went to an ATM machine. For some reason it didn't work. I returned to the table and told my colleagues what happened. I knew they would cover me, but before we ordered, the waitress came to me, and in excellent English, said that she overheard I didn't have money. I explained that my friends would cover my dinner.

But the waitress said, "You are in my country, you are in my city, and you are in my restaurant, don't worry, I will pay for you." I was blown away that she was offering to pay out of the kindness of her heart.

I assured her that I was OK and I just wanted dumplings, which my friends would pay. She then said, "You are a big man, and dumplings are not enough for you. I will get you lobster or steak and only charge you for dumplings." Her kindness and generosity impressed me. Needless to say, I didn't take her up on her offer. I thought she was in for a rude awakening if she encountered the ugly American tourists or individuals who would take advantage of her kindness.

But my encounter with this young waitress was not over here. Two weeks after I was in the city again and decided to stop by to have some of those delicious dumplings and say hello to my new friend. I ordered the dumplings, and since I was alone, checked my guidebook to plan some future excursions. The waitress came by with the food, and she looked upset.

"Put the book away," she ordered. "Our cook put his talent and his energy into making this food for you, and you disrespect it by not giving your full attention to the food. So put your book away and focus on your meal." I was shocked being chastised by this young girl. But I quickly remembered this girl's previous kindness. I then apologized and put away my book. This seemed to please her, and I ate my dumplings paying full attention to their delicious awesomeness.

Houzi

Before I ever went to China, I started to learn Chinese because I made friends from China who were living in New York. New York had very large Chinatowns in Queens, Manhattan, and Brooklyn, where the inhabitants spoke mainly Mandarin, many not even speaking English. I attended Chinese social gatherings and events, which fed my fascination with the Chinese culture. I met a Chinese lady who had a translator, and we had a delightful evening. I invited her to dinner, but her translator did not join us.

So my first question was, "Do you like Italian food?"

She looked at me with a quizzical expression and asked, "Italian?" Then I spent the next five minutes drawing a map of the world, pointing to Italy, saying Italy, Italian. She nodded, then asked, "Food?"

This was going to be a harder task than I thought. She had a little English dictionary in her purse, and I asked to see it. I quickly learned the verb to be and the phrase "What is this?" The very first sentence I ever spoke in Chinese happened when we passed a statue of a monkey.

I queried, "Shenma? (What is this?)"

She replied, "Houzi."

I then constructed my childish sentence. "I am a monkey" (Wa shu houzi). "You are not a monkey" (Ni boo shu houzi). How this poor girl didn't run away in a panic was a miracle. And that is how I started to learn Chinese, "What is this? What is that? What are those?"

Over the years, I picked up more Chinese, but I spoke like a child not worrying about proper tenses and tones. My vocabulary was also lacking. One day I was with ten Chinese speakers, and the weather was getting cloudy.

I then said in Chinese, "We should go indoors, the sky is going to cry."

"Oh, you Americans are so poetic."

"No," I replied, "I just don't know the word for rain."

So one day I was walking down the streets of XiAn. When I felt the tugging of the hairs on my arm. I looked to find a little boy pulling my hairs, saying *houzi* (sounds like house-za). You probably realize from the above that this little boy was calling me a monkey. Chinese don't tend to have hair growing on their arms, so I looked closer to a monkey than a Chinese boy. Another day I'm walking down the street and I felt the pulling on my arm hairs and heard again another young child say houzi.

"Yes, I'm a monkey," I replied. Then a third day, I felt again the pulling of my hairs on my arm. This time, to my surprise, I saw a short elderly man pulling on my hair and saying *houzi*. I guess if you're a monkey, you're a monkey.

A Cab Ride

Customs are different in different countries. For example it is very common to expectorate in China. It would not be uncommon to see a person spit in a mall. In fact, in some restaurants, they even have spittoons where the clientele can spit out their phlegm. A friend of mine was having dinner with some Chinese friends in Beijing. Now and then they would spit on the floor. My friend blew his nose into his handkerchief and then returned the handkerchief to his pocket. He then noticed that a few of his friends had an expression of disgust. For them it was disgusting to spit into a handkerchief and then keep it. They will release their phlegm to the ground but not save it.

One day two of my fellow English teachers and I took a cab to XiAn. On the way, the taxi driver kept bringing up phlegm as he was driving. I made an expression of disgust to my fellow passengers, opening my mouth and positioning a finger as if vomiting. At that moment, the driver spit out the window. My window was down, and his phlegm went out his window and back into mine…right into my mouth. Oh my gosh, that was disgusting! I was gagging. The spit was slimy and gooey. I started digging the phlegm out of my mouth with my fingers. One of my fellow teachers saw what happened, and she was in shock. The other kept asking what happened. I brought up my window, and he did it again; this time it dripped down the raised window, protecting me from getting it in my mouth again but getting a clear view of what had entered my mouth just minutes before. When I talk with my students about transmission of viruses, I mention how the most common way of transmission is by touching surfaces. Getting spit in your mouth is not a common mode of transmission, but it definitely would be a means of transmission. A student asked if I hit him after he spit in my mouth.

"Of course not," I replied. First of all, he wasn't calculating the angle by which the spit would enter my mouth. There was no ill intent. He was just doing what was customary for him. Secondly, he was driving, and it would have been crazy to assault our driver. Our driver wasn't sick, so I didn't get sick. Disgusted but not sick. This is one taxi drive I will never forget.

Parkinson's Dreams

In 2015 I was diagnosed with Parkinson's disease. This neurological disorder comes along with various symptoms. There is a saying in the Parkinson community that goes, "If you know a person with Parkinson's, you know a person with Parkinson's." In other words, each person with Parkinson's is different. Some symptoms are common, but the degree and the type of symptom varies from one person to another. For example I had tremors in my right hand but not in my left. In 2019 I underwent a Deep Brain Stimulation Operation. After the operation, my right hand no longer shook. Another symptom that is often related to Parkinson's is the occurrence of strange dreams. Once I dreamt I was playing soccer in a FIFA football game, which is strange in itself because I don't play and I am not even a fan of the game. In my dream, the ball was passed to me, and I kicked it to the goal with all my strength. Only in reality, I kicked the bedroom wall with great force, injuring my toe. My purple toe was a reminder of my Parkinson's dream. Another dream, which finished in an injury, was one where I was in an airport when an individual pulled out a gun. Without wasting a minute, I jumped the terrorist. But in reality, I literally jumped from my bed straight into a cabinet near my bed. I bounced off the furniture and onto the floor, hitting another wooden stand of an office chair. My face was swollen, and I spent hours icing my face.

Finally another weird dream was when I found myself fighting off zombie dwarfs (Too many episodes of *The Walking Dead*). They were overtaking me, and I fought my way, punching and kicking them. All of a sudden, I hit something soft.

Then I heard my wife say, "What are you doing?" Sure enough the last contact against the little zombie was right across my wife's face. Luckily it was more a brush than an Oscar slap. Whichever way, sorry!

The Bronze Medals

It was a long day of competition at the ISFL (Independent School Fencing League) team tournament, and after strenuous encounters, our girls' foil team finished off medaling in third place. The girls were so happy since this was this team's first time to make the top three. They all received bronze medals and they were ecstatic and so very proud as they received their third-place awards. Then something unexpected occurred.

One of our team members came to me and said, "Coach Rue, I could be wrong, but I believe there was a mistake in the calculations. We actually came in fourth place, not third." I told them I would look into it. I went to the directors' table, and after recalculating the results, there it was. My student was right, we were actually fourth place, not third. I went over to the coach of the team, which in reality won third place. He told me that he also saw the mistake but didn't want to say anything because our girls had already gone up to the podium and had received their medals. He was concerned for our girls. This was a very admirable attitude, but I knew something had to be done to correct this error. I went to our girls, who were gathered talking about it.

I explained the situation and then said, "Ladies, give me the medals, and I will give them to their proper owners."

For the first time ever, my fencers told me, "No." I couldn't believe my ears.

"What?" I questioned.

"No, Coach Rue, we will not give you the medals….we will give the girls from the third-place position their properly earned medals." Then one by one, the RCDS girls put the medals around the necks of the opposing fencers. They had tears in their eyes, and the recipients of the bronze medals were also tearing up. They hugged each other as the parents watched on also with tears in their eyes. I was so proud of them because I knew this had to be difficult for them, but it was the right thing to do. And the best thing was that it came from the fencers, not the coaches. On the bus ride home, I had the opportunity to speak to the team.

"Ladies, in a few years, nobody will remember who won third place, even first place. But everyone will remember the admirable actions of the RCDS girl fencers who bravely handed over the medals to the opposing team." The principal from the opposing team sent a letter to our school commending our fencers' behavior. At a full school assembly, our principal praised the female fencers for their actions and gave each girl a special medal for sportsmanship. In my thirty-five years of coaching RCDS fencers, this was one of my proudest moments and I will always remember the fortitude of these young fencers.

Marillion

In the eighties, I came across a German exchange student who introduced me to her favorite band, Marillion. I had never heard of them before, so I went to Tower Records and bought a live album of theirs, "The Thieving Magpies." I fell in love with this music. The lead singer was a Scot who went by the name Fish. His actual name was Derek Dick. In 1989 Fish left the band and was replaced by Steve Hogarth.

Fast forward it was in the decade of the nineties when one of my students came to my office and said, "Hey, Mr. Rue, I know your favorite band is Marillion and I thought you'd like to know that they are going to play at Toad's Place in New Haven, which is a relatively small venue around the Yale Campus." I thought that it was probably a cover band doing their songs, after all they would fill stadiums in Germany and England. But I decided to go anyway to spend a night listening to Marillion songs. So I was standing right next to the stage when Steve Hogarth and the band members emerged from behind a curtain. It was "them." The real "them." And it was a magical evening.

The Lord of the Rings

Another fast forward to the new millennium when I heard that Fish was giving a concert at BB King's on 42nd Street. I got tickets for my wife and me. This was another small venue making for an intimate performance. Fish was great. At one point, he came among the crowd as he sang one of his songs. When he approached me, he patted me on the head like one would do to a puppy. I thought this sign of recognition was humorous. Then my wife jumped over to Fish and gave him a hug.

All she said was, "He was sweaty!" But it was great fun interacting with Fish.

And this was yet one more connection to *The Lord of the Rings*. The band was originally called Silmarillion after the Tolkien book, but eventually the name was shortened to Marillion.

https://en.wikipedia.org › wiki › Marillion

My Philosophy

My experience studying in the university in Spain left a mark on me for the future. It molded me but not necessarily as you might think. My professors were inspirational but not in a positive way. I often felt that I was drowning and needed assistance, but they weren't available to help. I eventually finished my graduate degree with honors, but it was a very difficult experience. Once a teacher told me that he always enjoyed reading my papers....because he would get a good laugh. I remember thinking that if I ever found myself in a position of power as these teachers had, I would do everything possible to help those students who needed help.

After getting my medical technologist license, I worked in that field for a few years, but I wanted to try my hand at teaching. Fast forward into the future, I have been a science teacher for close to forty years. I truly loved being in the classroom and sharing time with my students. My subject was challenging, and there would be students who had difficulties with the material. This is where my experience in Spain kicked in. I remember swearing that I would not allow any student who wanted to succeed to fail. Any free period, before classes and after classes, I would meet with my students who had the need of assistance. To begin I would have the student explain to the best of their ability the most recent lesson. Like this I was able to gauge where their weakness was. Then we would go over the material, and I would fix any chinks in their armor. We would meet fifteen minutes every day and review the lesson until they felt comfortable with the material. In reality it was just letting them know that I was there for them. The rest would fall in place.

As it turned out, my experience in Spain was truly influential and beneficial to make me a successful and empathetic teacher.

The End

I must say that the end of my teaching career at Rye Country Day School was the topping of my teaching cake. After thirty-seven years teaching biology and forensic science and thirty-five years coaching fencing at RCDS, I decided to retire. It seemed to be a good time to reinvent myself and try new things, starting by writing this book. The students and my colleagues gave me an impressive send-off....actually multiple send offs. My colleagues threw a faculty party where they honored me with happy memories. The fencing team honored me, including a battle of light sabers by two of my fencers. My biology students gave me presents, including a number one issue of Web of Spider-Man from 1985, the year I started teaching at RCDS. My friends gave me a tribute at our Lobster Fest gathering. I was honored to be selected by the seniors to give a talk at the Senior Blue & Gold Dinner and a standing ovation at its conclusion. Finally I was moved by the presentation by the ninth-grade class in front of the whole student body. There were testimonies, including photos going back to 1985, video clips, and a salutation by Samwise Gamgee, Sean Astin. These students and my colleagues shared their warmth, love, and respect, making me feel ever so grateful. I consider myself to be a most lucky person for this.

Acknowledgements

There are so many people I am grateful to who helped me over the years. First, I am thankful for my parents and sister and her most amazing children, David and Crissy. Their intelligence and fun-loving personalities helped me through all my years and these experiences guiding me to write these stories. Thanks to my wife Misako for being supportive throughout this process. A shout out to my fencing buddy, Bob Boyer, who kept alive the passion for this sport and to Martin Schneider who was my Yoda, making me a better fencer and coach. Thanks to my childhood friend, Joe Murno, and his kids, who kept my chess skills tuned. A special thanks to Flora Rue for reviewing this work, adding punctuations, correcting the grammar, and adjusting the spelling. A recognition to my friends and colleagues from Rye Country Day School, who were always there for me. I am very thankful to the students I have taught and who made me love every day I showed up to school.